A COLLECTION FROM THE
INSTAGRAM POETRY COMMUNITY

Mosaic

AVA BALIS

MOSAIC
A COLLECTION FROM THE INSTAGRAM POETRY COMMUNITY

iUniverse books may be ordered through booksellers or by contacting:

iUniverse
1663 Liberty Drive
Bloomington, IN 47403
www.iuniverse.com
1-800-Authors (1-800-288-4677)

ISBN: 978-1-5320-7308-3 (sc)
ISBN: 978-1-5320-7172-0 (e)

Library of Congress Control Number: 2019904327

Print information available on the last page.

iUniverse rev. date: 04/15/2019

Contents

Foreword

The poets and creators featured in this anthology were asked to submit a work following only one criteria: that their work made them *feel deeply*. As creators, we seek to explore and express depths of emotion, and this anthology presents us with a wide array – a *mosaic* – of such depth through the various topics and angles explored within it. That is the beautiful thing about art: in art, we can take reality and hold it up at different angles – look into it through different lenses – and mix our deepest selves in with it. It was in wanting to give voice to many different creators, and all of their individual artistic perspectives, that this anthology was formed. The ability to create, and the ability to have your creations shared with the world, is important to all of us: we do not create only for ourselves, but rather to *share* our experiences and have them be understood in a way that, often, usual conversation does not do justice. Expression is an essential part of all our lives, and each unique perspective deserves to find a home for its voice. Thus, this anthology features 62 rising (and often first-time) poets and creators, sourced from Instagram's poetry community, all with a different take on what makes them *feel deeply*, and each with a different artistic style. These pages are a beautiful, diverse collage of passion, depth, and poetic and artistic talent that I have been proud to assemble. I hope you enjoy our creative mosaic.

- Ava Balis, poet and author

Translation

by Ava Balis
@ava.balis

I wish I could speak to you
from behind my words;
they are such
embarrassing, fumbling tools
sometimes.

Oh, just slide under my skin already;
I can't take this draft of silence
diluting the thick of all I want to show you but can't;
tearing nervous gaps in the
dance of our gaze.

I have...
so many colours you'll never see,
so many angles and contours
that flatten under the grid
of our limited dictionary.

And I want to show you my world
but it comes out
with the cling of silver;
tinny words

spilling out onto the coffee table
like cheap imitators.

Oh well.
Let's keep using these
dull tools
and someday,
as they sharpen against the steel
of whatever this is we're building,
we won't even need them.

OH JUST SLIDE UNDER MY
SKIN ALREADY;
I HAVE SO MANY
COLOURS TO SHOW YOU.

INTJ

by Jessica Wang
@alittlenotion

Note from the poet: *This piece marks the beginning of my poem series inspired by the Myers-Briggs personality system. I have long been fascinated by the meticulous workings of the human psyche and hope that through my words, I will be able to better navigate the many universes of human souls. The complete series can be found on @alittlenotion on Instagram.*

high tide rises as sun curves low
in an arc of perfect timing
saltwater laps, serenely climbs,
but recedes before my feet,
for i stand bold in the best plot
of sand to count waves and watch the sea,
and i hold truth in still, steady hands
through dirt and dust and dreams.
yet there are murmurs i hear deep in the night;
whispers sweet and strange and tempting

there are moments i squint towards
distant shores and
wild thoughts they flash—
they gleam:

how would it be to inch close enough to be shocked
and cooled by sea?
how would it be to soar fierce, cry out
through reason—grab chaos
and flee?

Awakening

by Tina
@pure.dedication.to.healing

The air was
thick like honey.
She knew she felt safe,
but she didn't know anything else.

With every breath
she became more and more
aware that she was part of
the Universe,
and the universe was part of her.

Lessons

by Stacie L. Seidl
@stacieseidlwrites

A repeated lesson learned
Strength builds when it is tested
Truth though slowly discerned
Resilience is manifested
Change need not be feared
Growth lies within its meaning
Courage persevered
The Universe is intervening

Prelude

by lydia falls
@lydiafalls_

piano fingers,
my mother called them.
long and thin
they'd dangle,
self-consciously
by my sides.
there was so much of me
i learned to call
endearing.
so naturally,
i longed that
you'd learn, too.

Rich Prices

by Giana Say
@giana.say

Bittersweet will always be in our fates
Harmonies in our paradoxes
We are roots without branches
Divided by oceans
Trying to build helpless bridges
We didn't burn down in flames
But all we have left are ashes
Our hearts are wild to love
But they grew inside cages
Lips feeling love and never tasting kisses
Eyes always screaming
While our mouths held wordless phrases
Emotions drown in love
But skin never felt enough touches
Our love was rich
But now we pay the prices

mother's arms

by Faren Rebecca Rajkumar
@faren_wanderer

bewildered
by the words of those who
feed me false scripture
who lift me up & throw me down
and prefer to be alone
but never are
I run to you
and I thank you, Mother
for accepting my tears
for once, lonely becoming
a comforting place
among your flowers & your falling sky
almost reborn
more shadow than woman
exactly as the Sun
intended me to be
somehow,
somehow, sadness
lives there still
and this is how I know
I am weak
but I am always alone, and braver for it

and will accept the kindness of praise
but only from you, Mother
for attempting to save my soul
I only wish
all the unseen love in my heart
was enough to save you, too

Honey, have a drink with me

by Amber Liu
@amberkliu

Honey, have a drink with me.
Right here, in my dying room I have like a sun, full
of bottles that clink like dead men's autonomy.
It's a good path through this lily neck of woods,
and when you walk away
the sky like yellow and haywood,
sick and straw gold.

Oh dear, don't look at me like that,
      like I know what I'm doing with my feet,
      like I bite things that aren't my tongue.
Don't leave me with these noisy demons
whose talk is rich with florid irony,
cheap and callous and coming undone like pearls.

Come inside to a dinner with one too many plates;
Put up with me your feet on the wooden mantle and forget
what it is when the house burns down and
the people still come home.
Let me rub you raw against the chafing in my laugh,
burning your half-moon mouth on black coffee and
asking you which clouds pair best with this brand of melancholy.

Have a bottle on me, my love:
        of poison, of tears, of letters and promises—
        of men as shaky as knobbed knees.
I am learning exhaustion as he visits me in the parlor,
pulling his shoulders over my clothes hanger frame
and dragging the cat back in to die.
There's a good place by the fire where I promise
you'll only burn if you want to.

So take a seat in this sinking, burning ship that turns at sea—
live the way love learns to drown in me.

To be like you again...

by Alexandria Rose Rizik
@alexandria_rizik

To my younger self —
why couldn't you stay?
I miss your naiveté,
I miss those easy days…

Remember when you didn't get
those dirty jokes? The ones all your friends made?
I remember.
I understand all of them now — and
sometimes I make them too.
Seems I've gone retrograde…

Do you remember
when having a crush was so pure…
and holding hands
made you feel so grown up and mature?

Can we go back to riding bikes
with friends?
And Friday
actually feeling like a gift… like the weekend?
I guess I'm wiser now.

And maybe I don't get as emotional
over the little things, like breakups and men...

*But I'd give anything to be like you
again.*

love revolution

by Nadia Lucassen
@nc.writing

the most beautiful
revolution
is the one
within yourself
when you find
the strength
to be more vulnerable
and become open
to feeling love(d) again

not love

by Vahitiare
@ amitalus

it's alarming
how quickly
i fell for someone
who gave me
breadcrumbs of love

you showed up
dressed in all the words
i didn't know i was so
desperate to hear

substituting sex
for intimacy
i got high on
your occasional
snippets of affection

so hungry for love
i took what
looked like it

rip out the remains and set them on fire

by r.d.b
@fromrdb.withlove

the way ivy grows on the Japanese maple outside this window
takes me back to growing up in the Appalachian foothills
how English vine would creep up the stone walls by my bedroom
my young mind saw only its beauty and charm
a storybook cottage
oblivious to its destructive properties—
that it was slowly pulling rock from siding. making a home
between layers. becoming one with the foundation. taking more and

more
space.
consuming.
undisturbed   no matter how harsh the winter.
parasitic.

sometimes ivy vines have people names
and you do not notice until years have passed just how deep
those roots spread

the house still has pale white scars from time spent
touched
by hungry, selfish fingers

The ghost of you

by C. H. Loe
@chloeiswriting

And just for tonight,
let me dance with the ghost of you
to remind me of
how beautifully dead we are.

untitled

by Diana Cristurean
@a_pen_and_some_words

i know what it's like to want the world
and to want it now
to want it all at once
the anxiety that gradually resurfaces
and makes you restless for the rest of the day
the feeling of needing to get out there
and do something
change something
make something new simply happen
for yourself, for others, or for both
or else you'll just lose your mind
internally combust
spiral down into an existential vacuum
that right there
all of that
is the calm before the storm
the flicker before the flame
it means you have plans, dreams, goals
that may be bigger than you currently have the capacity
to comprehend entirely

it's a good feeling, don't be mistaken
you should trust it, follow it
because it means you have in you the
desire to live

Reparation

by Priyanshu Mehta
@_the_little_notebook

Weaving in and weaving out
Thread by thread she'd go
Sewing memories onto her heart
Pretty patches to fix those holes.
Carving poems on her bones
And patterns candy-striped
Painting over your spills and splatters
Covering every single bit.

The nicks and the cuts,
All your traces on her soul
Yes, she encrusted everything,
With the gems she plucked
From her sturdy backbone.

Flowers bloomed as her sorrows
Dibbled into the veins.
And there were rainbows everywhere
But without the weary rain.

She built a doorway through her heart,
Fenced off from the ribs

A door so all the menace
Could easily be skipped.
A Door for those who broke in
But never longed to abide
A door to save the damage
And so, it's all for her to decide.
A door, so the ones waiting to be let in
Don't get to shatter her apart
A door, so it's up to her
Whether to answer your muffled knocks
Or just let you depart.

I say she's a work of art
And you here wonder why?
What kind of masterpiece needs repair, every once in a while?
Yes, I accept she's been in a damned state
And have been fallen through
But an artwork requires restoration to survive,
Isn't that also true?

Home

by mrs
@thatsmethebee

i am looking for
less flowers, more roots

Flowers

by Emily Stoddard
@emwrites_

Gradually, flowers grew
from inside my lungs—
a garden of everything
I wanted to say but never
had enough breath to.

Chest burdened with soil,
and a bouquet of words
caught in my airway—
it was beautiful, but
it was suffocating.

Falling Piano Keys

by B.A. McRae
@ B.A.McRae

The symphony grew louder in the back of my mind.
As my fingertips gently touch the black and white keys, the
sounds of the world were blind.
The rhythm flows through me and escapes into the atmosphere.
Each note so defined, each note so clear.
The beautiful melody played softly at its own pace.
But the symphony was stronger as my heart started to race.
The violins played faster as the cellos followed along.
The piano's keys tried to keep up with the song.
So powerful and mighty the rhapsody played.
Somewhere in the madness the melody had stayed.
The notes came out fast, faster than they had been.
A sudden shock from beneath me, as the tiles under me began
to cave in.
The stone crumbled so quickly, as the symphony became amused.
Support failed from beneath me, defeat I refused.
Gripping onto the keys as the base of the piano hit my knees.
My world collapsing around me as it hits my face; the falling
piano keys.
The adrenalin that matched the violas pitches so high.
The black and white keys falling on me as I closed my eyes.
Feeling the air hit my back as it begins to sting.

Such a feeling of falling in nothing.

But the symphony began to seem calm the keys no longer hit me.

Softly it was, but I could hear the melody.

Suddenly flashes of light I could see behind my closed eyes.

Like there was string around my wrists they lifted and were set down as they began to untie.

And to my amazement I see.

Lined up perfectly; the white and black keys.

The world lifted back in place, the symphony not a trace, has my world now attained?

Or is it the real question now, have I gone insane?

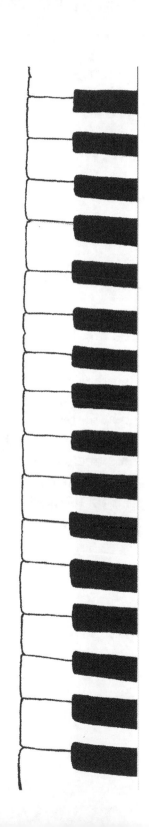

Hello, Goodbye

by k.
@lusciniapoems

You are the summer rain
in bright light nights
that kisses me into focused
insanities.
You are the bittersweet taste
from our chilly nights of heated
encounters.
You are the definite maybes
that fill the deafening silence of our
limited forever.

untitled

by ChaosKeep
@Chaoskeep

loud noise
eye catching
bright colors
like fireworks
in my mind
you're inescapable

In the Rain

by -andrew.pens-
@andrew.pens

I was lost.
Existing only
to feel time pass me by,
trapped somewhere
between the heartbeats
of a million strangers.
Alone, I tried to find life
in the faint laughter
of young lovers
dancing in the rain,
but instead
I was merely asleep
in another fading dream
to a better place.
And then
in the darkest day
you found me
standing by myself
in the middle of the street,
and you asked me
if I had ever danced
in the rain.

Luna

by Molly Moreton
@sol.et.luna.writes

A permanent smile,
She'd wear it
Like a crescent moon,
Grinning, she'd bear it
But that was as a child,
Carved deep into her quiet.
Now sometimes I see her,
A passing flash in
Windows and mirrors,
Her face turning sour
And that cherry red sheepskin
Still holds her close,
Still warms her bones,
Enduring their treacherous
Journey together,
Sun-faded, tear-stained,
Worn out and
Withered.
Ash and smoke,
Angst and hope,
Love received,
Too much delivered.

Too young to consider
Herself drained to the core,
Even with old songs engraved
In her soul.
I don't want her to look so cold,
Tired eyes, arms folded
And I know this will never
Last her long
Because she wants to heal,
Grow and blossom.
And so we will,
Ocean salt, daisies, snow -
We will climb the sky, blue indigo,
Find that Lantern of Lovers smile,
Return it to her lips
And watch her glow.

untitled

by mariam.j.
@mariamhassanj

Of all the things
I lost on you
love was my favorite one

Nights to Remember

by inkxflowers
@ inkxflowers

When our bones go brittle
I want to remember these nights
when you take my hand and run.
These nights when our laughter
chases down down echoes in alleyways
and whiskey traces our tongues
and smoke fills our wanting lungs.
When our hips sway and feet dance
until light breaks through the darkness
in the east, burning holes in our eyes
and with parched throats our heads pound
and lying on bathroom tiles we wonder
"Is this how it feels to die?"
I want to remember those nights
when it was just you and me
and our blind naivety.

Tinder

by Amanda C.
@skinandthoughts

In a world where
everyone looks for a match
I'm searching for the flame
knowing I might get burnt
if not in this lifetime then the next
but I will find you again

Timmy

by Catri
@ curiositykilledthecatri

Timmy was the Peter of his generation, stuck forever in his little Neverland, never wanting to grow up. He struggled in school with his t's crossed like r's and his r's crossed like t's. He was cherry blossom sweet but he was sly, so sly with the devil in his eye.

He became a navigator of great trickery with a cheeky smile as his aid. He copied the girls work, word for word and didn't even bother to change it. And he rode upon the arrogance of the boys.

School was his playground and he was not on route to change that. Timmy was stuck, stuck forever in his little Neverland. Timmy never wanted to grow up. Never ever ever.

He was cherry blossom sweet but he was sly, so sly with the devil in his eye. If angels could fly down, they would fly away. Away they would fly, chasing shadows until the days were out.

Timmy, Timmy, when would he ever learn?

Never, never, he was stuck forever in his little Neverland, never wanting to grow up.

Timmy, Timmy, when would he ever grow up?

Timmy didn't want to, he really didn't want to. He was Timmy. He was cherry blossom sweet but he was sly, so sly with the devil in his eye.

Where there's a will there's a way, and Timmy found his way. Master of manipulation, navigator of great trickery with a cheeky smile as his aid. His days were numbered, numbered they were but believe it he wouldn't.

Life After You

by Diosa de Agua
@diosadeagua

My life after you
Isn't as bad as I once thought
If there's one loss in this tragedy
It's actually you, who lost me entirely.

Regret

by Jasmin Lacoste
@sacredinblue

You're tasting like regret
And I'm enjoying the flavor,
Your eyes an ever changing color.
This isn't butterflies, its fear
Stop pulling me in,
Moving on slowly,
But you're always in the back of my head.

Sunday

by J.R. Mason
@jrmasonpoetry

Sunday
sounds like the tiptoeing
of juvenile blackbirds
between two pock-marked walls,

Smells of bonfire smoke
and ransacked moorland,
Calfskin gloves and
dog-eared aprons on a barbed fence.

Sunday
is a dull Tanglewood guitar
in the hands of a sponge
in a sooty-black bedroom,

With a latent voice
like grit and glue,
Deep as the entombed shafts
of a forgotten colliery.

Sunday
is a garden fork

resting in a sodden alley
stained with drunken beatings,

It is flea-bitten knees
and scrawny Europeans,
Blood on the Tracks
and Belgian beer.

Then Monday,
A pumping vein bleeds
for a band of vole-eyed girls
in uniform,

And away again,
Away again,
Away again,
A penny drops.

Wolf

by Sian RJ Wilmot
@srwpoetry

OH,
YOU HAVE THE TALE TWISTED,
I AM NOT WHAT YOU THOUGHT.
YOU HAD ME DOWN AS A DAMSEL?
DARLING, I'M THE WOLF.

A longer distance

by Simthandile Lisakhanya Witbooi
@ignited_by_blue

An elastic is stretched across the sea

How far does it go
when it's made of -
difficulties solidified,
the human spirit,
Resilient, Flexible

Sensed in a chemical
suspended over cities
A connection forging
Over unseen sights
attracting despite the
petrol and fuel in between

hollow
our hearts are leaning forward
no matter how hard we stretch
space remains

Chewing me up
leaving me soulless,
the absence of you

An elastic stretches over the sea

And
it

Snaps

untitled

by Casee Marie
@hopeandharbor

I want the mountains,
steepled in a wild sky
and the spark of the fox's eye
and the knife-edge of the eagle's wing
and the call of all living things,
not by mere heart's desire,
but by the soul's demand.

Enough

by Grace E. Stevenson
@susurruspoetry

I am the owner
of endless half
written letters
unfinished thoughts
ideas never brought
to fruition
words that die
on the tip of
my tongue
as if there is a
mouth more
worthy of
uttering them;
But only I
can finish this
sentence and
it will be
good enough
because
I am good enough

Depth

by Lauren Taylor
@the_world_soul

i've stripped down
bare boned as
the winter trees,
naked in my truth,
past lives,
and narratives
for you to read

but you refuse to
interpret anything
beyond the first page

i am so much more
than the
surface swiftly scanned

The Shift

by Ashley Marie Egan
@darlingashez

Once I was the prey
a furry cuddly little thing,
but my innocence suffocated when you
crushed my windpipe between your jaws,
you told me shy girls whet your appetite
with a charming smile and thirsty eyes,
then like a leech you drained my will
until I felt weak, no, replaceable,
but my blood has run cold
and like a snake I will shed,
the wretched past
crusted and dead,
until my scales shine anew
then I will move on from you,
and never again will I be blind
to predators in disguise,
the way I was with you
for I've become one too,
but we are not the same
for I turn predators into prey.

Bears & Weeds

by Ri Robinson
@ ri_robinson_writing

Did you know that magic still exists.

Did you know that there are bears with blue-grey fur.
Fur the color of murky ocean waters.
Fur the color of thundered skies, like deep indigo and greying
slate.
Almost dead
All of them
But not

All of them.

Did you know that glacier bears still walk the earth. That magic
still walks the earth.

Maybe poetry will never solve any problems.
But, I'd ask you, have you ever seen a poem, some words –
help a person grieve
help a person heal
make a person

whole.

I've seen it.

Did you know
that in your ruins -
In your weed o'er grown despair -
There is beauty where the ivy spreads.
There is magic

even there.

& if the grass begins growing black, well then the grass will still
be growing.
There is sureness in uncertainty
Deep grace
within the hoping.

Did you know that magic still exists in
bears & weeds
and like
bears & weeds,
it walks & grows.

There are some moments that are magic

Like,
when a woman is told that something is not made for her
& she adds it to a list of things that she will make herself.

Like,
when a child is told that the color of their skin means they will
never be pretty
& they decide that they will be beautiful, instead.

They say we are what we eat
So I think

If we feed ourselves poetry
Then that's what we'll become

I hope

That it's what I'll become

Like magic

Like a weed

One more glacier bear
With ampersands as feet.

I hope you
Know
That magic
Is exactly how we write it

And Maybe
Only
when we write it

If you look long enough
for poetry

You'll find it.

mountain mansion stories

by Stef
@stefpoetry

swallowed up by the throat of a mountain
into the wild I must go.
here stalagmites and stalactites lull
crystals to good nights;
there are fairies bearing twig-tousled hair,
exchanging poise for cozy rosemary air;
turn up your eyes and castles have sprouted wings,
their roots flout and float away with royals' wedding rings;
down, down we go to run with miles of rivers,
who've become ballroom floors for ages of lavish lordly lovers;
somewhere around I've seen turtles and tigers fed with fairies'
dust,
now they're singing sylvan hymns sitting atop wind gusts;
and in all the cardinal corners, smiles are hung to sway as oil
paintings,
the fairies, the rivers, the royals;
they've built a mountain kingdom where secret, surprise, and
serenity are reigning.

into the wild I have gone,
inside the wild I'll live on.

Courage

by Aarbe
@silly.aarbe

Blooming

by Emily Rose Hinz
@thethoughtblossom

she is soft
and rigid
broken
and loved
ever growing
and ever beautiful

the depth
of her strength
is not something
that was given,
it is something
that was fought for

one day
you will see
it is not your own worth
you should question
it is whether or not
others are worthy enough
to hold your heart
in their hands

you are
divine, female
gracefully mending
shattered pieces
and turning them
into peace

untitled

by the.poets.daughter
@the.poets.daughter

she knows how much I need her
when I need her the most
so she fills my life
like the stars fill the night sky
my solace,
my saviour,
solitude

I fell in darkness with you

by gizem.yasemin.cevlik (wild.ribbons)
@wild.ribbons

The deeper I fell in love...
As much as I struggled to get out...
I realized that nobody
But you could save my soul.
How ironic was it?
You were the one who placed
My passion into darkness,
And you are the one
Who could armor it too.

And one day,
I lost my butterflies that once winged; inside of me
But they left diamond pieces puzzled on to my hair
With wild ribbons tied to my heart,
My sentiment lost a beat every time I took a breath.

ptsd lullaby

by marissa valenzuela
@mvpoesia

antidepressants
   for thoughts heavily weighed
      the sun shines through the darkness
         not for me, not today

awake when I sleep
   asleep when I wake
      it is all real, all the same
         he has come back to cause pain

3am nightmares
   cold tears and puddles of sweat
      I do not know rest
         but exhaustion, yes

there is no mercy, no safety
   nobody to come save me
      four soundproof walls
         nobody hears me screaming, nobody hears my call

he has me trapped
   chained to my shame
      my very own father
         his own DNA

I spent five long years imprisoned
   my soul suffered silently
      he made his way rightfully
         onto the sex offender registry

there will never be justice
   regardless of his sentence
      I relive the abuse daily
         forever captured in its essence

It's All About Perspective

by Estel
@estelpoetry

/Pessimistic says/

I will always be 'that' victim
So, don't tell me that
'This is just a phase that will pass soon'
Because I am aware of the truth.
My wounds go too deep for time to heal
And
My heart is too numb to feel
I will never truly believe that
I can rise from the ashes.
Because I am convinced that
The time has sealed my fate
And
I have already got enough on my plate
So, I can never accept that
Everything is going to be fine.

/Optimistic says/ (Now read bottom up)

perennial

by Nina Prabhu
@honeytohive

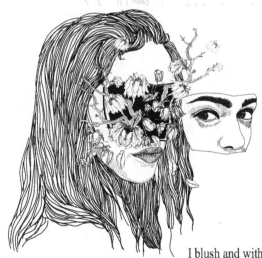

I blush and wither with the seasons,
and steal the light that spills from his sun.

yet, his soul is always in bloom for me.
and for that, I am forever his.

hive

Everland

by Zora
@feuerzora

Imagine a land
where no one has to cry.
Where it's always night,
you're stuck in a beautiful dream.
Where fireflies shine bright,
warm and yellow.
A land with a violet sky
and sparkling hills
where fields of poppy bloom.
A land without fear
and anger
and hate.
A land where the plums taste sweet.
Imagine a land
where no one has to cry.
Everland.

Vulnerability

by She's The Thorns
@shes_the_thorns

She was undeniably beautiful
yet something about her
was so tragically sad
she would never let me
explore her depths
she would rather drown
in the shadows of her mind
than expose herself
to vulnerability

nor believe me
when I said
I wasn't here to judge
but to accept it

@shes_the_thorns

I'm Jealous

by Britney Villa
@b.v.writing

I'm jealous of the birds flying in the sky so free
I'm sitting on the ground watching the world move
as I am stuck
Though the world spins I find myself unable to move
I'm jealous of the rain
how it falls
wherever it wants to
It can cover a whole street and no one will tell it not to
The wind caresses my cheek teasing me
with its ability to dance
its ability to be cold or warm
I'm jealous of the wind
I'm jealous of the rain
I'm jealous of how the world moves
how it never stops moving
Maybe someday
I'll learn how to be one with mother nature
so I could move
so I could choose
so I can dance
and no one will tell me not to

a colorful love it was

by renee wolf
@heyreneewolf

i was blue, only blue.
and you were yellow
with just a touch
of blue in you.
and together we made
the most brilliant green
i had ever, ever seen.

Breaking the Broken

by l.a.h.s.t
@l.a.h.s.t

It will never be the one who tore you to pieces that will piece you together again.

Please stop reaching out for his hand to help you up while it is his foot pressed across your chest keeping you down.

Grieving and Letting Go

by h.e.r.
@itspouringwords

I am too tired to keep it all inside-
that i begin to give my body a chance to-
grieve,
and grieve,
and grieve,
Until it feels safe to breathe again,
and i can tell my reflection in the mirror,
"You are a survivor."

an almost-love story for the winter months

by Rhan Ireland
@rhanireland

i. *the beginning*: i first met you in a city of ruins / during the beginning of cold winter days / you sloped into step beside me / i smiled at you / and that was it

ii. you messaged me good morning / you put kisses when you said goodnight / you reached into my insecurities / and pulled them out raw

iii. you called me baby / darling / *my love* // we had silly pet names for each other / i still can't think of that word without my muscles tensing

iv. i was heady with infatuation / constantly on the best kind of edge / waiting for you to reply

v. you didn't wish me happy new year / perhaps i should have seen it then / i was too in love with the idea of love / too obsessed with the ticking of the clock / to stare down the truth

vi. *the middle*: on our first date / i wore red lips and tight jeans / you turned up late / i made most of the small talk / we split the bill / you didn't message me afterwards

vii. more hours, more days, more silence

viii. the first day of class / you walked in / looked at me / and sat several rows away

ix. the trees were consumed by frost / the good morning texts stopped

x. i wanted so much more than you were ever prepared to give

xi. i lapped up your honey-tipped lies like nectar / always desperate for more / more / *more*

xii. you carved out my heart like the core of an apple / twisted the knife until it drew blood

xiii. *the end*: i would rather have a beaten-up heart / than be someone without a heart at all

electricity

by cb
@camilleblaispoetry

Isn't it lovely how
our bodies light up
to the current
of our love
how with
every touch
and every smile
we can illuminate
entire cities

Naked

by Megan Fulton
@poetrybymeg

I want to touch you
Where no one else has
The places that are unexplored
Bare and raw
Where no past lover has been
I want to dwell
Where sometimes you don't even go
The lost corners of your mind
Where your hidden desires and demons lie
Begging to be left alone
I want to welcome them with open arms
And dance with them
Each night until the sun comes up again
So I can swallow you whole
And leave no piece unturned
To be fully naked
With each other
And watch our love grow

untitled

by Lourdes Montes
@lou.m.art

Note: the painting attached to this poem is titled "joyeux".

My heart has a memory of its own
Left over traces of passion and trauma
That pull strings on my body
Hopelessly
Inevitably
I glow or isolate
Based on my heart's fears
Based on my heart's desires

And the world transforms in front of me.

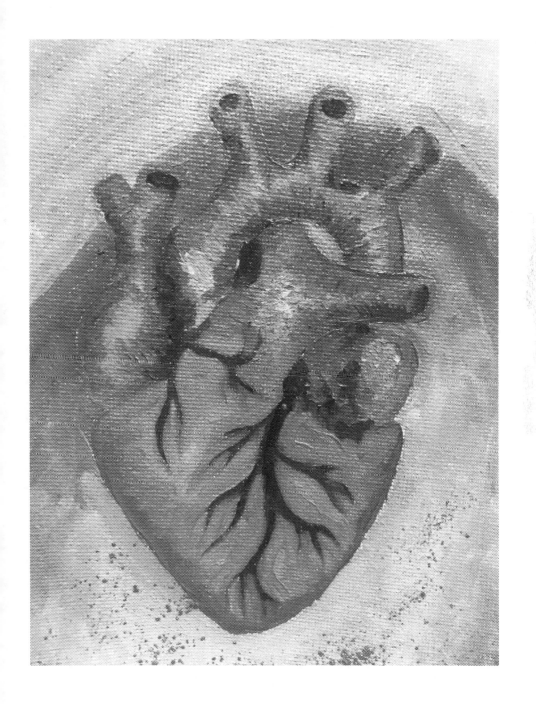

Poetry

by Euphonic Poetry
@whispering_euphoria

And this october, the forest demanded
iridescent galaxies, imbue art,
drowning cosmos, and nefarious stars.

Everything felt like an unearthly passion,
embodied in me like a flower
growing out in eternal bloom season.

As if my ethereal heartbeat rewiring
itself to beat to a new poetry song.

When I looked at you, my enticing eyes
bloomed roses, sunflowers and pink skies.

When you touched my skin, carnations
as well as peonies grew like leaves.

When you kissed my lips, thousands
of daisies exploded from my mouth.

I never knew, how you make
my garden grow with such beauty.

But you were the one, the only one,
who could turn my heart into poetry.

Farmland of Fleeting Escapades

by Madhuwanti Ghosh
@thegoodbadwords

I was told that when you can't fall asleep
You should try counting sheep jumping over a fence
I imagine a big green farm, and always a broken brown fence
The sheep jump over, one after another, as I count.
One. Two. Three…
The sun is brighter in this farm than it is elsewhere
"But the sun only comes out when it feels like coming out."
I see Holden Caulfield sitting on the grass
Next to my sister, who is busy untangling my thick black hair
She is upset because I made us late for the bus again
Oh the dreaded missed bus! I run.
Familiar, endearing sites pass me by
Scribbled school bathroom walls
Lost pieces of jigsaw puzzles
Birthdays, Anniversaries, Hand-Crafted souvenirs of a life almost lived
Piles and piles of unopened wishes
Memorised train routes
Dried flowers pressed between discoloured pages of poetry

The night I heard Chopin for the first time
I run faster. Still searching.
Crossing abandoned sheds, emptied to make room for someone who never came
I sweat longing, longing filled with 'what ifs' and 'If onlys'
I stub my toe against the edge of shameful desires running down the insides of my thighs
It hurts, an accustomed pain
Like burning myself on scalding tea while carrying it to the living room
Burnt skin
Cold toilet seats
Itchy mosquito bites
And there it is.
The wrinkles on the side of his eyes when he smiles.
The wrinkles on the side of his eyes when he smiles.
The wrinkles on the side of his eyes when he smiles.
One. Two. Three... And I sleep.

The child in me

by Breshna Abdul Hadi
@breshnawrites_

When she was a child,
she danced in the rain,
as though nobody was watching.
She let the winds touch her soul,
as her heart soared through the blue sky.
She left smiles on everyone's faces,
growing gardens where the remains of their sorrows found a home.

When she was a child,
happiness chased her,
even if she ran away.
But she grew up too fast,
she forgot her moves
and instead of the winds,
she battled storm.
People forgot her,
and happiness found a way to escape.

And perhaps,
maybe,
she was faster,
and ran a little too far.

Mars & I

by [blue]
@bluewritinghere

i,
   as mars,
   am a planet
   to discover,
   to reach out to,
   to figure out.
   and i commit myself to be,
   my own astronaut

String Theory

by Emkay Walter
@emkaywalterpoetry

There's no such thing as 'poor timing',
for we're all pawns of fate.
I have no use for 'early',
I don't believe in 'late'.

In multiple dimensions
with infinite design,
I was meant to be here,
and it's the *perfect* time.

untitled

by Gabriela Lino
@gylwriting

You could see the whole world through her brown eyes,
like looking into a kaleidoscope, a reflection on each side.
Beautiful masterpiece she created
using her mind.

dry mouth

by A.D. Galatis
@_paperthin_heartstrings_

some words
get stuck in our teeth
and rot in our throats
the fear of letting them slip
keeping us
from allowing
hearts to drip
from our lips
never believing
another
would ever
thirst for a taste
of our truths
assuming
they'd rather die
of dehydration
than drink us in

untitled

by L.T. Pelle
@L.T.Pelle

My god is tender and moony,
only when the night is quiet
and elegiac blue
do I release her from between my hands.
Only then do I release her.
Everything I hold is a dream,
everything I hold waits inside me
with ready wings.

Beacon

by Lourdes Montes
@lou_m_writes

From the best to the worse of my days,
you are the blessing that prevails.
The strongest beacon of love
that guides me out of the storm.
And love, I'm an island,
you are too deep in me to go.
You are the flame that sparks love in my heart,
A fighter of shadows sent from my past.
I learned of joy with you,
on stormy or sunny days.
I wake up to see the world with wide eyes,
ready to take in the colors it gives.
Because of you, I know kindness,
so how can I be kind to someone else?
Love is indeed contagious,
let me paint the world tonight.

Printed in the United States
By Bookmasters